Points of Departure

Other Poetry Collections by Miller Williams

A Circle of Stone (1964)

So Long at the Fair (1968)

The Only World There Is (1971)

Halfway from Hoxie: New and Selected Poems (1973)

Why God Permits Evil (1977)

Distractions (1981)

The Boys on Their Bony Mules (1983)

Imperfect Love (1986)

Living on the Surface: New and Selected Poems (1989)

Adjusting to the Light (1992)

Points of Departure

Poems by Miller Williams

University of Illinois Press
Urbana and Chicago

Publication of this book was supported by a grant
from the Illinois Arts Council, a state agency.

This book is printed on acid-free paper.

Library of Congress Cataloging-in-Publication Data
Williams, Miller.
    Points of departure : poems / by Miller Williams.
        p. cm.
    ISBN 0-252-02142-8 (alk. paper). —
    ISBN 0-252-06451-8 (pbk. : alk. paper)
    I. Title
PS3545.I53352P651995
811'.54—dc20   94-26824
                                                CIP

Acknowledgments

Many thanks to the editors of the following publication, in which some of these poems have appeared.

Hudson Review: "A Tenth Anniversary Photograph, 1952"; "Clutter of Silence"; "Lay of the Badde Wyf"; "Living Will"; "On the Sacrifice of a Siamese Twin at Birth"

Image: "God"; "Beside an Open Grave . . ."; "The Sense of Loneliness . . ."

Kenyon Review: "Holiday Inn"

New England Review: "Sleeping with Friends"; "Muse of the Evening"

Southern Review: "A Visitor's Guide to the Blue Planet"

Sparrow: "Deadsong for a Neighbor Child . . ."; "Six Lines Probably in F-Minor"; "The Consolation We Find in the Nature of Things"; "The Manifold Usefulness of an Education"; "To One Who Went Too Far"

Voices: "Fred"

And a very special thanks to Carolyn Brt and David Baker, who know why.

for Jordan

Contents

III

I

Going Deaf

No matter how she tilts her head to hear
she sees the irritation in their eyes.
She knows how they can read a small rejection,
a little judgment, in every *What did you say?*
So now she doesn't say *What?* or *Come again?*
She lets the syllables settle, hoping they form
some sort of shape that she might recognize.
When they don't, she smiles with everyone else,
and then whoever was talking turns to her
and says, "Break wooden coffee, don't you know?"
She puts all she can focus into the face
to know if she ought to nod or shake her head.
In that long space her brain talks to itself.
The person may turn away as an act of mercy,
leaving her there in a room full of understanding
with nothing to cover her, neither sound nor silence.

How We May by Chance Pronounce the Unsuspected Residence of a Ghost

I lifted a glass to get the waiter's attention.
"I'll be there directly," she said
across two tables.
One shade-spattered moment there was a backyard,
a woman in what we used to call a wash dress
calling from the kitchen,
with one elbow holding the screen door open,
drying her hands.

Getting Close

This is not some stranger you're talking to.
You know I know how almost every day
doing the ordinary things you do
you've seen my grin and not quite turned away,

when you were peeling an apple or changing a fuse
or moving the hair dryer away from the water.
You can think of me as a kind of muse
to help with the list of things that no longer matter,

or think of me as the circumstance unforeseen—
the siren dying in the still neighborhood,
the kitchen, the bedroom, the bathroom unnaturally clean.
I could make it stop hurting. You know I could.

At the Children's Hospital in Little Rock

Scorning the schemes of nature,
by accident, illness, and murder,
chance hands the past our future
and ruins us out of order.

We hope and beg as we can,
tugging the hem of frost
as if we were children again:
Us first. Let us be first.

The Consolation We Find in the Nature of Things

To understand that everything is happening always,
when next you're on the interstate at midnight
a little too tired to drive and you see something
for less than a second move on the highway ahead,
a shape in the darkness, a glint of the moon on metal,
don't squint and tell yourself it's a trick of light.

Say instead it's a '37 DeSoto
pulling back onto the gravel that use to be there,
a girl of seventeen sitting up straight
glancing at the illuminated clock,
pushing back her hair and smoothing her skirt.

They're always there as you are always there.

When you come close, that many years apart,
you see them there because your brain is idle
or maybe because you see your grandmother
or her grandmother, depending on when you read this.

How Did You Ever Live without It?
A Peppermill with a Light!

How, indeed? For some do die without it.

The couple out of gas on the wrong county road,
the gray-skinned woman sleeping on the grate,
the miner, trapped and trying to lie still—
who heard from each of them the hopeless prayer
for someone to come in time with a peppermill?

But now a climber, lost on a steepening slope,
sees a dog pawing heavily toward him,
bellowing hope across the blue drifts.
The dog stands above him, panting white pillows.
The man squints to believe. The wood looks right.
He puts forth a hand, the freezing fingers
nearly afraid to close on the polished oak.
"Thank God, thank God," he says, seeing the light.

Six Lines Probably in F-Minor

Though we have found some comfort in how the whole,
being more than its parts—read spleen and liver—
seems to make an argument for the soul,

still we could be nothing but star-stuff
recycling itself atom by atom forever.
The question may be why that is not enough.

A Tenth Anniversary Photograph, 1952

Look at their faces. You know it all.
They married the week he left for the war.
Both are gentle, intelligent people,
as all four of their parents were.

They've never talked about much
except the children. They love each other
but never wondered why they married
or had the kids or stayed together.

It wasn't because they knew the answers.
They had never heard the questions
that twisted through the jokes to come
of Moses and the Ten Suggestions.

They paid their debts and never doubted
God rewarded faith and virtue
or when you got out of line
had big and little ways to hurt you.

People walked alone in parks.
Children slept in their yards at night.
'Most every man had a paying job,
and black was black and white was white.

Would you go back? Say that you can,
that all it takes is a wave and a wink
and there you are. So what do you do?
The question is crueler than you think.

Home Young from Europe with All New Underwear

And just a bit sententious?   Judas Priest!
Or "Jeu d'esprit," as the French would say. At least!

Muse of the Evening

"I know I'm not the first," I said one night,
"but tell me if I'm the best you've ever had."
Suddenly she looked a little sad.
"You're not the worst," she said. "Shut up and write."

Sleeping with Friends

To have someone of compatible mind
lie down with her in disarray
is not to love, but she is resigned
to a hole in the heart she never can fill
and the couple of things she knows she can find—
the needful heat that will not stay,
the independent cold that will.

To One Who Went Too Far

No use to look for signs of old affection.
Some roads run in only one direction.

Raising a Glass to a Passing of Some Importance and Coming to Terms with the Limitations of Art

Oh Laurel, oh Hardy, oh Spanky, Hal Roach is dead,
who let us live in a world as if it were,
the better to be at home in the world that is.
Who've seen ourselves in both say, "Thank you, sir."
So what if we never know what Joseph and Mary
did with the gold and frankincense and myrrh.

Fred

Taking a husband's duties to heart
he kept her decently dressed and fed

and everything had seemed alright
till pissed again by something she said

and truly believing in the right
he whomped her up aside of the head

the way he had for all the years
they'd shared a table and a bed.

To his surprise she didn't cry
but turned and walked away instead,

went upstairs and got his gun,
took careful aim and shot him dead.

She stood with neither grin nor frown
and gazed upon him while he bled.

She managed to get him into a chair
and got herself a needle and thread

and closed the hole in the cambric shirt.
Then she got some jelly and bread

and milk and tuned the TV
to something she'd often wanted to see.

Deadsong for a Neighbor Child
Who Ran Away to the Woods

She finally found a place they couldn't find.
She wouldn't come if she could hear them call.
She knew love tore at the flesh, and flesh was all.
Stilled in breeze-blown stems and out of mind
she rode the buzzing summer, fretful fall.
She finally found a place they couldn't find.
She wouldn't come if she could hear them call.

Safe at last, unfeeling, deaf, and blind,
she lay past even peace, where countless small
and many-legg'd and legless creatures crawl.
She finally found a place they couldn't find.
She knew love tore at the flesh, and flesh was all.

On the Sacrifice of a Siamese Twin at Birth

We are one but we intended two.
Together, together we would surely have died.
Or worse, lived. Now one of us, one of us may.
But pity the hand whose closing scissors decide.

Living Will

I now, being of sound and light aware
and busily here but planning not to stay,
ask on behalf of a man who will use my name
that nobody when he is leaving get in the way,
forcing minutes and hours into his veins,
getting their long needs confused with his.
There is a time to think of who we are,
to call a thing precisely what it is.

When he's not his anymore, if there are things
in working order, take them as small good-byes.
Maybe the nose. He has smelled the crocus
under snow. Not those poor ears or eyes.
He won't care, but bits of him scattered around
will say that he did, if anyone cares to know.

Don't let him hurt a lot if you can help it.
Otherwise, be pleased to let him go.
When all the signs point off to you-know-what,
clear him a path. If he should need a hand,
he will appreciate it a whole lot
if somebody gives him one—if not as a friend,
for simple reason or pity, then only to watch him
twisting free of the same loosening knot
that holds you to your bones, in case you forgot.

Aubade

Quick, let's make love again. The apparent glow
from where the sun was eight minutes ago
is burning away the days. There are not enough
for learning much more than how to love.
Adrift among the planets, we think we show
some signs of knowing more than what we knew
when we began, then suddenly we're through.
Life is a brief and accidental gift.
The day we met is showing a red shift.
Ahead of us the emptiness is blue.

Catch with Reuben

You took for gospel what I said,
holding the glove
in just the way I said you should.
Knowing I never could teach you enough,
I thought that when you understood
how carelessly moments disappear,
your mind might hold, from a distant year,
a fading day and us still here.

No matter that your legs are short,
your arms are small,
it will all be right in time.
This arm that never threw a ball
far enough to make a team
if more than nine came out to play
threw one into your hands today
from nearly sixty years away.

The Manifold Usefulness of an Education

for Sarah and Sam and Charles
in school too far away

Geometry tells us how to tell
how far grandchildren are from here,
though this is not its only use.
It splits an angle down the middle
and calculates the hypotenuse.

Languages teach us of ancient words
with meanings like "stay" and "live" and "measure"
that hide in words we use today,
words like "distance" and "circumstance"
and "leave" and "love" and "months away."

History shows us how it was
before it became the way it is
to help us guess at what it will be.
Likewise it gives a reason to go
and sit in the shade of the family tree.

There is no subject that isn't us.
We learn, if we study with all our hearts,
that learning has a number of uses
beyond alphabets and angles
and rhymes and dates and hypotenuses.

The Sense of Loneliness in Spite of Everything

Oh, this is a time for not taking no for an answer,
a time for venturing forth, for finding out.
When faced with all the hypotheses and theories
explaining the origins and the ends of atoms
and time and space, we have to give grateful attention.

To think, for example, that once in a time before time,
when nothing had come to be but the center of nothing,
that point of infinite mass and no dimension
blew greatly apart to create light and weight;
that math and telescopes tell us there is a chance
time could turn back to that. This is a wonder,
an excellent thing to consider,
but it isn't something we know. What is, is this,
that we are no nearer to finding the face of God
in our endeavoring day
than people who painted beasts in the caves of France
and raised up stones to mean what they couldn't say.

A Visitor's Guide to the Blue Planet

Welcome to what
we kill and take
and lose and tell
and mark and make.

But Time will be a confusion
till you see parents and friends
fall to their separate ends.
With neither *will be* nor *was*,
you'll live in the present tense.

You're stuffed with days. They leave you slowly.
You'll pay no mind if people say
you'll come to feel the sun slowly
start to speed them on their way.

One day when you're naked in front of others,
playing after a bath, you'll suddenly know
—as if it were biblical knowledge—you shouldn't show
your flesh in that way, laughing, anymore.
You think you never will. You will, though.

One day you'll find yourself alone with someone else
when something not wholly your head will say, "There never was such
a mouth as this," and so you kiss and so you touch.
You'll learn there ever were such. You'll learn it again and again.
Learning will bring a sort of sadness, but not much.

Sometimes the present almost disappears
in all the up and down of the working years—
now is a place where *was* and *will be* meet,
but oh the *will be* and the *was* are sweet.

Then you'll notice something slowly.
Increasingly, you'll look around
a room, thinking of other things,
and be uncomfortably aware
that, maybe excepting a shadowy man,
a shawl in his lap, asleep in a chair,
you are the oldest person there.

Then they'll give you the shawl.
The old man won't care.
And you can have the chair.
You can have it all

till late or soon
some numberless year
there enters the room
touching your arm
one with a small
translucent voice
to say, "They're here.
They want the shawl."

Lay of the Badde Wyf

Part the first

All that she did she did not aim to do.
What she did intentionally was talk.
She had a simple hunger to say something
and see a sign that what she said was heard
by someone else, who might say, "Well" or "Maybe"
or nothing at all, but have the look of someone
to whom some words had recently been directed.

Home was where she watched the heavy hours,
each with its foggy number, grinding by.

She wanted once to work outside the home,
helping someone out somewhere for nothing.
Her husband said he would not hear of that.
She wanted once to have the kids by now.
Before the next promotion, though, and the next,
her husband would not hear of that at all.
She wanted once to join some other women
and take a morning walk around the mall,
but knew that he would never hear of that.
Her husband didn't like her being alone
with people he didn't know. Preacher, doctor,
woman down the street, it didn't matter.

She spent the day reading and running errands,
taking clothes to the cleaners and planning dinner,
paying bills and watching talk shows.
Sometimes, at night, she could imagine words
dying inside of her, empty of all their meanings.

Part the last

He ran the dry cleaners and lived above it.
"You couldn't say," he said, "it's much of a home."
She couldn't tell you why she went upstairs,
or when exactly. One day she was there.
She was surprised to see that she was there,
with new furniture and older music,
and pictures of people she never asked about.

They came with coffee first, the few stray words,
then cup by cup she told her whole life,
such as it was. And then he told her his.

She climbed the stairs repeatedly, to find
slower talk and coffee every time.
Then one day she took a glass of wine.
Then when she let his finger trace her lips
she felt something fall that she couldn't catch,
the way you feel it when you've dropped a plate.
Inside a held breath you hear it break.
All you can say is, Well, there goes a plate.

Not watching her body being released to the light,
not talking, either, she thought about her husband,
and what she was doing, and how to carry the fact,
the knowledge of it home, to make it a part
of pancakes and bills and looking for car keys.

Then she smiled, lying back in the light of her thoughts,
suddenly seeing how ascending the stairs
and drinking the wine and being naked there
would surely be among the numberless things
he himself would say he'd never hear of.
So let him never hear, for who was she,
unfaithful wife, to doubt his wisdom now?

Beside an Open Grave the Mind
of the Young Preacher Comes Almost to Terms

They know what they came to hear, he says to himself.
They're circling now for sure and certain knowledge.
If I can tell them nothing but what I know,
I can begin by describing my present discomfort
and tell them in closing how to spell my name.

I want to tell them what they want to hear.
If what they want to hear may not be true,
there's truth enough in knowing they want to hear it.

How are we sure of so little after so long?

Stop this stuff. We need a requiem here.
See, now, how silence pours from all their faces.

Well, then. Open your mouth. Begin. Begin . . .

. . . So let us begin to pray.
All language is requiem.
Someday someone will grieve
for us who grieve today
and then someone for them
as class by class we leave
where none could dare to stay.
Not for us to condemn,
defend, or beg reprieve,
or praise too much, but say,
O Lord, receive. Receive.

II

Jonathan in Awe

Jonathan walking, careful of every crack,
pausing to watch the supper traffic pass,
works through the list of mysteries in his mind:
that teakwood, when it breaks, will shatter like glass;
that no one knows from where the music came
to which we sing the words of *Amazing Grace*;
that no one is ever told what anyone tells;
that God, in the beginning, had only three ways
to express Itself—make nothing, or something else,
or make all this, where Jonathan saunters once.

At breakfast alone he thinks of how it is,
that when he is near the woman that he wants
with only a gnomic hope to raise its head,
he feels soprano, naked, and two feet tall.

Such are things of varied immediacy
that hold the mind of Jonathan in thrall,
no matter how much he longs for the mayfly thoughts
he had as a child to return and busy his head
when he is walking, stepping over cracks,
or pulling the blankets up on his narrow bed.

Jonathan Entertaining

Jonathan has invited all his friends
and says to those who come and lift their glasses
a second time for an old year as it ends,
a first time for a new one, "How time passes!"

He adds for conversation how one spends
the first gradual years, slow as molasses,
knowing nothing of what the world intends,
the middle years discussing gains and losses,

the later years not talking much of gains,
a bit of the victories children's children win,
but mostly of holding steady against the pains
of coming to terms and coming apart within.

Leaving, his friends do as they've done before.
Shaking hands and shaking heads together,
they pause two by two at the open door,
agreeing that life is hardly worth the bother,

leaving the wadded napkins, splattered floor,
the broken plate to Jonathan, who would rather
have eaten a mouse than stand a minute more
to watch each woman go and a man go with her.

Alone, he half suspects they *don't* agree,
not one, as if he'd shown a slide show
of a trip to places they didn't want to go,
with towns and mountains they didn't care to see,
and didn't have the heart to tell him so.

Jonathan Confronts the Question

He knows there are those who say you can never know
and he'd always assumed that this was true,
but exceedingly sad one night he suddenly knew
that God set up the whole thing for show,
then saw he had no one to show it to.

And now so God won't have to have the same
old audience all the time, we have to die,
filing out of the rows we occupy
more or less in the order in which we came.
Wave as you will, you'll never catch his eye.

Jonathan Losing

They cheered when he started out and kept it up,
took his colors and wore them as their own.
Go, they said. *Go.* He knew as soon as he failed
that he could have done it if they had left him alone.

Jonathan Happy

He'd never—though he saw the failing—
truly understood
how to know if he was feeling
bad or feeling good,

the former seemed so like the latter.
He laughs to know he sees,
pouring out a bag of litter,
spraying for ticks and fleas.

Heating his soup, he likes to keep
an eye upon the creature
curled on the arm of the couch asleep.
He loves their common nature,

that neither has anywhere to go,
both apparently willing
to rest in silence with things they know
that neither is skilled at telling.

Jonathan Seduced

He doesn't know what she wants or why she stays
as one by two by three the crowd thins.
He holds his folded papers and says, No,
he doesn't always know when he begins

where he might end up. Her, too, she says,
although she's practically done nothing at all
compared to him. What happens after that,
or if she tells him her name, he can't recall,

except for blinks of time, strobe-like scenes,
hands everywhere and flashes of long flesh,
almost like photos in all those magazines
he looks at when he has to. A suddenly fresh

expectant face, far from a circle of friends,
may make him remember where the memory hid,
and sometimes going to sleep, but he mostly intends
to know that it never took place till it never did.

Jonathan's Secret

Jonathan doesn't know how to tell a lie.
It's a handicap. He doesn't know how to say,
if anybody says, Do you like this thing?
when he doesn't at all, that he likes it anyway.

He knows that people think of him as honest.
In this he feels dishonest. Truth to tell,
he thinks he'd like to lie. He thinks he envies
people who do it sparingly and well.

He puts the words together but they won't stay.
It looks like shit, he says. He never intends
to hurt anybody. He'd lie, if he knew how,
his tongue loose to have some faithful friends.

Jonathan in Mourning

Beside the grave, a bottle in his hand,
Jonathan tells himself that from the start—
not giving a thought to where the thought will land—
from even before the murky pulling apart

of autocatalytical carbon rings,
till suns reclaim their planets in the end,
nothing happens twice and most things
never happen at all. "I don't intend

a eulogy here," he sighs, squatting down.
"A brief configuration has fallen away,
and what is less dependable than a noun?"
Lifting his bottle up to the fading day

he thinks about how barely he is here
and brings the bottle down for a long drink.
Bushes around the yard come darkly near
as the air turns chill and he watches the sun sink.

He says to the bottle, taking another pull,
"It's strange that anything is anywhere . . .
it's sad to feel what I felt when you were full,"
and forms what might have been heard as a kind of prayer.

"Lord knows it was law, back before things began,
that everything that is, is the only one,
a cat as unrepeatable as a man,
so now there are reasons enough and now there are none."

He thinks that tomorrow he might cut back a little.
Trees are creeping toward him across the lawn.
He drains the last swallow from the bottle.
"I've got to go in," he says. "Poor Kitty. Poor Jon."

Jonathan Aging

Jonathan feels like a character out of Dickens.
He's served foods he can't digest anymore.
He feels things move that never have moved before.
His graying hair grows thin and his body thickens.

He thinks of mortality more than he used to.
He knows his friends have seen how his flesh is soft,
that he has neither time nor interest left
to do the few things that he used to do.

He finds time for another glass of scotch
before dinner, is still surprised to hold
the paper so far away and misread his watch.

If it confuses him how people grow old
to curse the lapsing of the heart and crotch,
it was never a secret and he was certainly told.

Jonathan at Last

He thinks of when he is dead and how it will be,
of how a colleague could say, or maybe a neighbor,
being by every convention laudatory
within the limits of truth and good grace,
that if there was little enough of grandeur and glory
still he suggested something of Rome and Greece.
Or, failing that, someone could rise and say
that he was often remarkably civilized
for a man who lived alone in constant dismay
in a large house where couples came to the door
prepared to tell him why they couldn't stay;
who had a cat, as brief as it was small,
and once a brittle hope, briefer than that,
and little help or comfort ever at all.

III

The Young Instructor Talks to Himself
Winding Up the Semester

So then she will go away. And what's the loss?
Thinking of love is more and loving is less

than we have wanted to say. So let her go.
Someone twisting her hair in the back row

will take her place, one with benevolent lips,
her eyes at times betraying a little lapse

of what she calls attention, vaguely gazing
into the middle distance. You will be praising

her lips and hair and eyes in the same bed
where each one seemed to put her pretty head.

Again when morning comes she'll sit in class
twisting her hair to make the minutes pass.

You'll think this time she might almost recall
the sass, the nakedness, the long caress,
but you can see in her eyes that she doesn't at all.

Clutter of Silence: Invention for Two Voices

You ought to see him there in the backyard
standing like a stump. About sundown,
he wanders out and tosses a rock or two.
A squirrel could nest in a pocket and he wouldn't know it.
He used to tell me what he'd done all day.
I'd let him talk then tell him how I felt,
the sun going down, but he would never listen.
The day his sister died he crashed the car
so he could know that he was feeling something.
Nothing seems real to him till he acts it out.
We haven't laid down for love in a long time.
We didn't do it together when we did it.
Not really together, I mean, him looking down,
me looking up, the ceiling fan turning,
his body telling both of us when to stop.
Do I still love him? I'd like to say I do.
I worry about him when he has to travel.
I guess I'd worry about anybody
that shared a house with me for thirty years.
Does he love me, though? That might be the question.
He sits for hours without saying a word
and never likes anything I fix.

You ought to stand where I do, out in the yard.
Watch any window and there she'll be, in the bedroom,
lights off and on, the dining room and kitchen,
like if she sat for a second something would get her.
She thinks I don't pay attention but I do.
When I get home from work I always ask her,
What did you do today? and she says, Nothing.
Doing, doing, all the time doing,
and never caring to tell me what she does.
She gained ten pounds of grief when her mother died.
That's when it came to me like a bumper sticker,
her flesh is just feelings in disguise.
It never had a purpose all its own.
We've come to not make love much anymore.
She doesn't care and I can live without it.
We did it once the way the movies do it,
but then she started watching the ceiling fan.
Do I love her? Who else might I love
if I don't love her? We're talking thirty years.
You could turn that question around to her,
who gets mad with no warming up
and puts oregano on everything.

She Talks to Her Sister, Briefly By
on the Way to West Memphis

It's been four years now, come October five.
You're sure you won't have another bite?
There's plenty more. I did look forward to it,
the day he wouldn't have to go to work.
But listen to me. Not even getting married
can change a life like having him underfoot.

That's him hammering something in the basement.
He's built himself a workshop, thank the Lord,
else he'd be here with me all the time,
talking and talking with nothing to talk about.

There aren't a lot of things that need repair
about a house like this, the two of us,
so we end up—I guess a little surprised—
reading the newspapers, eating in silence,
and finally talking again in spite of ourselves.

It wouldn't behoove me at all to fault him for this.
He's doing what we planned for him to do.
He truly is the salt, you know, of the earth.
There's not a negative thing worthy of notice
that I or anybody could say about him.

Years ago once, when I was doing the laundry,
I found a phone number stuck in a pocket,
a local number in someone else's hand
written on the edge of a paper napkin.

It was the napkin set my nose to itching.
Half of me didn't want me to but I called it.
A woman said hello and I hung up.
I didn't know what to say. She might have been
the wife or daughter of one of the men he worked with.

Well, that was back a long time ago.

The time when people ought to be together
night and day like this, day and night,
are those first years, when nothing seems enough.
Not now, when a brushing touch can do for a day.

What this does, you know, it makes it harder
for one to go on alone when the other dies.
You get too used to being half of something.

He traded himself in for what he's got.
I suppose it shakes some wrinkles out,
stopping a way of living and starting another.
I wouldn't know. I'm doing the life I've done
for more than forty years, except that now
I can't talk to myself the way I did.
He thinks I'm talking to him, and I ought to be.

Sometimes I think, Who is this person I'm wearing?
I can't recall the last time I sat
and stared at the wall as long as I wanted to.

Still, I know, I might have spent those years
with some sad man who lacked imagination
to know the difference between the truth and fact,
who never said, when he heard a siren start,
that someone's plans for the day had come undone.

Listen. Here he comes. He'll want to show us
something he's put together or taken apart.
He'll want to set it down where we can see it.
Sometimes it is remarkable what he does.
I think he thinks that everything is fine.
I've never said a word of this to him,
so you can see now what the problem is.
If he doesn't have the good sense to see
that I don't care for anything anymore,
including him and whatever he has in his hands,
if he doesn't have the sense to see that,
what is he going to do if I die first?

Jonah on His Deathbed

I was ready long before this day.
You've read that I was, but save for the barest facts
you don't know half the story from where I stood.

It wasn't hard to see why He picked me out.
I was a good Jew and free to travel.
Also, being a prophet—though I grant you,
not well known till all this came to pass—
I was prepared to see the ways of God
and make them known in well-crafted phrases
the Lord would lay in my mouth. I'd done it before,
on small assignments, and done it very well.

Most of the time we saw eye-to-eye,
but why the Lord should attend to Nineveh
was something I thought deserved a little discussion.
I made a list. For one, the Ninevites
are ignorant. For two, they're happy so.
For three, they pose a constant threat to peace.
If that was not enough, I meant to mention
what an embarrassment to humankind
they are, whose only art is arrogance.
And what would other prophets think about me
running off to visit such a people?
Would anyone believe that God had sent me?
Of course He did! And can't you see them grinning?

I failed to see what good it was going to do.
"Tell them I'll overthrow them," He said. Sure.
"A month and ten days," He said. Right.
Then He'd probably spare them, whatever happened,
and there I'd be, looking like a fool.

So what the heck, I thought, a little side trip
till He gets interested in something else.
Maybe Tarshish, down the coast of Spain,
a little mining town run by Jews
who surely needed to hear the word of God
and had at least the blood to understand it.

I only had to go as far as Joppa
to come on a foreign ship prepared to sail.

I was sleeping the sleep of a clear conscience,
two days out and not a word from the Lord,
when the storm hit. The sailors woke me up.
I can tell you they were terrified,
the sky black and the sails about to rip.
Up on the deck we cast lots, to learn
which one among us God was angry with.
Can you believe it? There on a lurching ship,
breakers nearly as high as the creaking mast,
each of us shaking a bunch of chicken bones.
Of course they pointed to me every time.
I wanted to say they had rigged the whole thing
but I knew better. I knew what I had to do.

God would have drowned the lot of them to get me.
He doesn't have to answer to anyone,
but I was not about to stand before him
with twenty drowned Phoenicians on my hands.
I told the men to toss me overboard.
I lacked the nerve to jump, and on that count
I'll thank you not to judge.

                              I have to say
I saw more compassion in their eyes
than I had heard in the voices of the Lord
since this began. They bent themselves to the oars,
which I took as a kindness and still do,
but soon it was clear that I would have to go.

Wrapped in the fish, I knew what he wanted to hear,
but I think I was madder than he was.
I decided I wasn't going to say it.

There in the slime, though, the smell and the darkness,
I said the words. I said, "My Lord, I love you."
I said it twice again, and He let me out.
And then I got myself to Nineveh.

You can imagine that I was in no mood
to hold forth. I told them what He said:
"You've all got forty days, and that's it."
Then every one of them saw the light at once
and went home and changed to sackcloth.

I half-suspected God was playing games.
The king heard, and he ordered the people to fast.
Also, the dogs and donkeys and cattle and sheep
were not to have any food or water at all.
They also had to go in sackcloth.

God said they seemed a nice bunch of people
who demonstrated remorse and He wouldn't hurt them.
I knew that's what He would say and He knew I knew it.

I can tell you, it put a strain on things.
I yelled and tore my clothes. "Go on," I said,
"and finish me off." Then I got out of there.
I walked as far as I could. When it got too hot
I settled myself down on the side of a hill
to see if the Ninevites would mess it up.
That was where He truly became unkind.

First, a gourd grew up and blocked the sun,
which at first I took as a nice gesture.
But then He sent a worm into the plant
and the plant died. And then the sun and the wind
bore into my brain. "Just go ahead and kill me,"
that's all I said. The Lord spoke in thunder,
"What have you got to be so angry about?"

That's the line that did it. He knew well enough.
I slapped my forehead and tore my clothes some more.
Then He said, "Look. Try to feel some pity.

These Ninevites are not very smart,
and think of all the cattle I would have killed
if you had not come and I had striken the land."

Sure, I thought, and what about dogs and sheep
and donkeys with no water for more than a day?

But, as the story is written, I did not answer.
What could I say, sitting there in the sun?
That this was all for show and out of fear?
He loves them both.

                              I truly meant to die.
He wouldn't have it. Who knows the ways of the Lord?
Perhaps it gives Him pleasure to have me here
telling this story again. What else can I do?
Think what it's like with half your life to live
and known as the one who used to be the prophet
that God chose to send to Nineveh.

So much for me. You want to know something else?
After the squeezing gut, after the stink,
three days inside the fish, after the awful
courtesy on the ship, what I think of most
are the animals under that sun, with nothing to drink.

At the Sanity Hearing He Speaks
in His Own Defense

The truth is, you don't want to understand.
Doing what we've been assigned to do
becomes important when you think about it.
To look as if I don't know how I look
and never letting on how well I know
the meaning of things, the socks in the kitchen drawer,
becomes important when you think about it,
or watching water circle out of the sink,
which, if you think about it, means nothing at all.

They never see the strings we drag behind us
that tangle when we talk to one another
unless in leaving we unwind ourselves,

the finger always moving in the pocket
to keep the strings from getting so twisted up
that God has to lean down and cut us loose
or say, "Oh, hell!" and brush us off the table.

Coming Out

How could I have told you except to tell you?
I half-suspected you knew for a long time.
We wear each other's clothes. You must have known.
I thought you'd say, So let me call the papers,
or something like that. I'm sorry. I did it badly.

I thought the only thing to worry about
was how my folks will take it when I tell them.

My father can't even bring himself to believe
I'd want to love a man, much less a woman.
I'd give the whole world to have them tell me
it won't make any difference, but it will.

Even to you it does. You're afraid of me, right?
OK, you're not. You want a medal or something?

Hey, if you cry you're going to make me cry.
I told myself I wouldn't. So here we go,
both wet again, two kids at a frigging movie.

So look at this. Imagine how you'd feel
if almost everyone you knew was gay
and everyone called you queer if you were not,
if all TV and novels and billboards
had women loving women and men, men.
Think of telling someone you wanted a man.

My father will leave the house and sit somewhere.
My mother will go into the kitchen and clean something.

Remember when we hung around the high school
talking with all the girls about the boys?
I would go home and hit my hand with a stick
to make it stop wanting what it wanted.

Then gradually you learn to say the word.
The first person you have to tell is yourself.

Then more and more, whenever I lied to hide it,
it was only the lying I was ashamed of.

So don't think I don't like myself. I do.
You're never going to make it if you don't.
Imagine saying every day in the mirror,
Shame on you. What if your parents knew?

I've thought about my parents a long time
but finally I thought about their daughter.

When I was little and I was all dressed up
for church or something my mother would look and say,
"You're going to make somebody a fine wife."

"Just put those thoughts away," my father would laugh.
"She'll never have to hunt for board and bed."
He'd lay his paper down and give me a hug.
"Are you going to leave your daddy for some other man?"
Maybe he can remember that now,
how happy it made him feel when I shook my head.

Holiday Inn: Surrounded by Someone Else's Reunion He Comes to Terms

for George Haley and the others

The large marquee said, Welcome Family Winston.
One N was upside down. Nobody cared.
From nearly black to almond, stroller to cane,
with license plates from Pennsylvania to Texas,
they filled the pool and parking lot with laughter.
They filled the lobby and both the elevators.

I made small conversation with a few
who might remember singing some of the songs,
holding a while a hand as white as mine.
Most who were younger than that, whenever I spoke,
shut their faces down and turned away.

One man with hair like gray-white rolling clouds
spoke kindly once. I left him to such a silence
I thought of old pictures, collaborators in France
ostracized and having their heads shaved.

As if I had not marched, and ridden, and sat,
and held hands and sung. But what should that buy me?

I had a dream in which a black child
said, "Papa, all those people look the same."

I won't say they were for nothing, the years together.
Lord knows we lost, but it was a good game.

Showing Late Symptoms She First Tries to Fix Herself in the Minds of Her Children

I try to take them where they want to go
but not to let them have their way too much.
I try to play their games, but not so much
I make them uneasy, making a fool of myself.
I cook what they like when I can. I tell them I love them.
I tell them too often, though, and they don't hear me.

If there's a chance that one of them might remember,
it won't be the baby. His brother's six and a half.
The little one won't be five for seven months.

But then I've thought, If I could plant something
that might come to blossom far in the future,
if I could find an odor, something rare,
something they might not smell on anyone else,
something no teacher or friend's mother would wear,
if I could afford it, then maybe in twenty years
one of my sons would say to some young woman
in some distant city, "Nothing. It's nothing.
Something made me think about my mother."

Wouldn't that beat all, me suddenly there?
Not knowing of course or caring, but still there,
a kind of ghost, just floating in the room.

They're still so young, though, their hands are so small.
I don't want to haunt them. They're wearing my flesh.
They'll cry me slowly away at bedtime.

But that would be something, the woman pretty and all.

The Old Professor Fast-Forwards
His Last Lecture and Goes Home

We stopped last time as Europeans began
to look this way, their seaports full of the sound
of ships being built, because an Italian man
with a Spanish flag, who thought that he had found
the coast of India had, true to plan,
shown a skeptical world the world was round.
Another Italian had come before he came,
by stars and luck and farther up the way.
Now we call two continents by his name.
The other has towns, a country, and a day.
Also a sadly declining reputation.
But each is secure in the books as first to reach
America, the mass of land. The notion
that grew to be a country where the rich
and wretched were not always born so,
and think of living by law and compromise,
is still being discovered—slowly, though,
as few by few we raise up our eyes
and see our names written in the Bill of Rights,
scattered letter by letter, but clearly there.

A word of possibility invites
a sentence of hope. But hope can spoil the air.
Nothing rotting in a basement smells
like hope gone bad. It is by guts and law
and love and luck hope grows to something else
in places like Fort Smith and Saginaw.

Few of us here have traveled hard or far.
Most are here by birth and some by chance.
Others, descended from others who long before
came here by choice, indentured, or in chains,
still gather uneasily inside invisible gates,
lugging with them color, habit, and speech
in pride and exhaustion. Nobody else waits
as long or travels as hard or far to reach
America, America, as those
we call the first Americans, who lost
the bridge they crossed from Asia—no one knows
how many millennia back—then wandering, crossed
a warming continent and walked to its end,
then stood and watched Columbus walk ashore,
and lost the land they found and came to spend
their shrinking lives contending over a share
of what was theirs. And many women, too,
study and wait. And some who are sick, and some
whose bodies collapse, or senses misconstrue,
and some who otherwise have misbecome.
And some who loving lie upon their kind,
and some who are simply ignorant and poor,
still grope to find America, to find
a light to set a path by.

Blood has made sure
a lantern is held high. Even so,
the outnumbered, the sorely afflicted, the old,
can find it hard up close to catch the glow
so visible far away. The story is told
of a cobbler once becoming so intent
on making shoes and money that he was lost
in awful concentration when he bent,
as every day he did, to leather and last.
With money he was as free as he was proud,
throwing coins to children on the street,
but died a metaphor, who had not allowed
for time and leather to shoe his children's feet.

Some still discover America, every day
laying claim upon it. But it may take
more days than many have to find their way—
even, say, for sweet history's sake,
with ancestors urging them on, in Swedish, Greek,
in Athapaskan, Czech, Swahili, Russian—
as they invent continually what they seek:
the old dream that once became a nation,
an old nation still becoming the dream.

This is what we mean by coming true:
the being is in becoming. Though we seem
to stumble backward, doing the things we do,
upon that fear itself a hope can feed.
The dream is coming true when all of us know
it comes too slowly true, and then proceed,
and see and care how far there is to go.

That's it. Wake up. Go forth, do well, and breed.
Give some thought to how your children grow,
and some to the long connection of need and greed
to both old quos, the status and quid pro.
This is complex. If anyone gets the grade
an answer deserves, I'd be the last to know.

Publisher's Note

Back in 1964, when Miller Williams and I had thirty good years ahead of us that have slipped by in a hurry, I was pleased to have the opportunity to publish his first book, *A Circle of Stone*, as the first poetry collection from the Louisiana State University Press. He has written a lot of poetry since then and I've had a hand in publishing a lot of poetry. It is a particular pleasure to get connected with Miller again, not only for old time's sake but also because he's one of my personal favorites.

"For Robert, Son of Man" was the first poem in that first book and it seems appropriate to make it the last poem in this new book.

Richard L. Wentworth

For Robert, Son of Man

With eyes that have found the rain and first stars
you looked from your face to my face
Robert . . . son
What are these for?
your manhood held in your fingers
where frogs and rocks were held
in the wild yards.

Then your great things were boulders coming down
tumbling from some cold and holy place
What are these for?
loudly through centuries
to find me here in this Buck Rogers town

this year in this Roy Rogers room, with you,
holding your name, looking at my long look
What are these for?
I'm full of lies to tell
to a boy of five, half-Christian and half-Jew.

Rolling from where it tumbled when you spoke
the answer comes ochre and smelling of earth
and we are together
in a circle of stone
where the sun slips red and new
to a stand of oak.

MILLER WILLIAMS, University Professor of English and Foreign Languages at the University of Arkansas as well as director of the University of Arkansas Press, is the author, co-author, or translator of twenty-seven books, including eleven poetry collections. He has received a number of literary awards, including the Henry Bellaman Poetry Prize, the Amy Lowell Award in Poetry, the New York Arts Fund Award for Significant Contribution to American Letters, the Prix de Rome for Literature and the Academy Award for Literature of the American Academy of Arts and Letters, the Poets' Prize, the Charity Randall Citation for Contribution to Poetry as a Spoken Art, and the John William Corrington Award for Literary Excellence.

Illinois Poetry Series

Laurence Lieberman, Editor

History Is Your Own Heartbeat
Michael S. Harper (1971)

The Foreclosure
Richard Emil Braun (1972)

The Scrawny Sonnets and Other Narratives
Robert Bagg (1973)

The Creation Frame
Phyllis Thompson (1973)

To All Appearances: Poems New and Selected
Josephine Miles (1974)

The Black Hawk Songs
Michael Borich (1975)

Nightmare Begins Responsibility
Michael S. Harper (1975)

The Wichita Poems
Michael Van Walleghen (1975)

Images of Kin: New and Selected Poems
Michael S. Harper (1977)

Poems of the Two Worlds
Frederick Morgan (1977)

Cumberland Station
Dave Smith (1977)

Tracking
Virginia R. Terris (1977)

Riversongs
Michael Anania (1978)

On Earth as It Is
Dan Masterson (1978)

Coming to Terms
Josephine Miles (1979)

Death Mother and Other Poems
Frederick Morgan (1979)

Goshawk, Antelope
Dave Smith (1979)

Local Men
James Whitehead (1979)

Searching the Drowned Man
Sydney Lea (1980)

With Akhmatova at the Black Gates
Stephen Berg (1981)

Dream Flights
Dave Smith (1981)

More Trouble with the Obvious
Michael Van Walleghen (1981)

The American Book of the Dead
Jim Barnes (1982)

The Floating Candles
Sydney Lea (1982)

Northbook
Frederick Morgan (1982)

Collected Poems, 1930–83
Josephine Miles (1983)

The River Painter
Emily Grosholz (1984)

Healing Song for the Inner Ear
Michael S. Harper (1984)

The Passion of the Right-Angled Man
T. R. Hummer (1984)

Dear John, Dear Coltrane
Michael S. Harper (1985)

Poems from the Sangamon
John Knoepfle (1985)

In It
Stephen Berg (1986)

The Ghosts of Who We Were
Phyllis Thompson (1986)

Moon in a Mason Jar
Robert Wrigley (1986)

Lower-Class Heresy
T. R. Hummer (1987)

Poems: New and Selected
Frederick Morgan (1987)

Furnace Harbor: A Rhapsody of
the North Country
Philip D. Church (1988)

Bad Girl, with Hawk
Nance Van Winckel (1988)

Blue Tango
Michael Van Walleghen (1989)

Eden
Dennis Schmitz (1989)

Waiting for Poppa at the
Smithtown Diner
Peter Serchuk (1990)

Great Blue
Brendan Galvin (1990)

What My Father Believed
Robert Wrigley (1991)

Something Grazes Our Hair
S. J. Marks (1991)

Walking the Blind Dog
G. E. Murray (1992)

The Sawdust War
Jim Barnes (1992)

The God of Indeterminacy
Sandra McPherson (1993)

Off-Season at the Edge of the
World
Debora Greger (1994)

Counting the Black Angels
Len Roberts (1994)

Oblivion
Stephen Berg (1995)

To Us, All Flowers Are Roses
Lorna Goodison (1995)

Honorable Amendments
Michael S. Harper (1995)

Points of Departure
Miller Williams (1995)

National Poetry Series

Eroding Witness
Nathaniel Mackey (1985)
Selected by Michael S. Harper

Palladium
Alice Fulton (1986)
Selected by Mark Strand

Cities in Motion
Sylvia Moss (1987)
Selected by Derek Walcott

The Hand of God and a Few
Bright Flowers
William Olsen (1988)
Selected by David Wagoner

The Great Bird of Love
Paul Zimmer (1989)
Selected by William Stafford

Stubborn
Roland Flint (1990)
Selected by Dave Smith

The Surface
Laura Mullen (1991)
Selected by C. K. Williams

The Dig
Lynn Emanuel (1992)
Selected by Gerald Stern

My Alexandria
Mark Doty (1993)
Selected by Philip Levine

The High Road to Taos
Martin Edmunds (1994)
Selected by Donald Hall

Theater of Animals
Samn Stockwell (1995)
Selected by Louise Glück

Working Classics: Poems on
Industrial Life
*Edited by Peter Oresick and
Nicholas Coles* (1990)

Hummers, Knucklers, and Slow
Curves: Contemporary Baseball
Poems
Edited by Don Johnson (1991)

The Double Reckoning of
Christopher Columbus
Barbara Helfgott Hyett (1992)

Selected Poems
Jean Garrigue (1992)

New and Selected Poems,
1962–92
Laurence Lieberman (1993)

The Dig and *Hotel Fiesta*
Lynn Emanuel (1994)

For a Living: The Poetry of Work
*Edited by Nicholas Coles and
Peter Oresick* (1995)

Other Poetry Volumes

Local Men and *Domains*
James Whitehead (1987)

Her Soul beneath the Bone:
Women's Poetry on Breast
Cancer
Edited by Leatrice Lifshitz (1988)

Days from a Dream Almanac
Dennis Tedlock (1990)